STEM IN THE REAL WORLD

ROBOTICS
IN THE REAL WORLD

by Robin Koontz

Content Consultant
George A. Bekey, PhD
Research Scholar and
Distinguished Adjunct Professor of Engineering
California Polytechnic State University

Core Library

An Imprint of Abdo Publishing
abdopublishing.com

abdopublishing.com

Published by Abdo Publishing, a division of ABDO, PO Box 398166, Minneapolis, Minnesota 55439. Copyright © 2016 by Abdo Consulting Group, Inc. International copyrights reserved in all countries. No part of this book may be reproduced in any form without written permission from the publisher. Core Library™ is a trademark and logo of Abdo Publishing.

Printed in the United States of America, North Mankato, Minnesota
082015
012016

THIS BOOK CONTAINS
RECYCLED MATERIALS

Cover Photo: Chip Somodevilla/Getty Images
Interior Photos: Chip Somodevilla/Getty Images, 1, 24; NASA, 4, 6; US Marine Corps, 9, 45; iStockphoto, 10; SSPL/Getty Images, 12; Underwood Archives/Getty Images, 16, 43; Ralph Crane/The LIFE Picture Collection/Getty Images, 19; Harlingue/Roger Viollet/Getty Images, 15; David Paul Morris/Getty Images, 20; Shizuo Kambayashi/AP Images, 22; Mark Ralston/AFP/Getty Images, 28; Red Line Editorial, 29; Alan Diaz/AP Images, 32; Haruyoshi Yamaguchi/Corbis, 35; Yoshikazu Tsuno/AFP/Getty Images, 36; Andreas Rentz/Getty Images, 39

Editor: Arnold Ringstad
Series Designer: Ryan Gale

Library of Congress Control Number: 2015945542

Cataloging-in-Publication Data
Koontz, Robin.
 Robotics in the real world / Robin Koontz.
   p. cm. -- (STEM in the real world)
 ISBN 978-1-68078-043-7 (lib. bdg.)
 Includes bibliographical references and index.
 1. Robotics--Juvenile literature.   I. Title.
 629.8--dc23
                                                        2015945542

CONTENTS

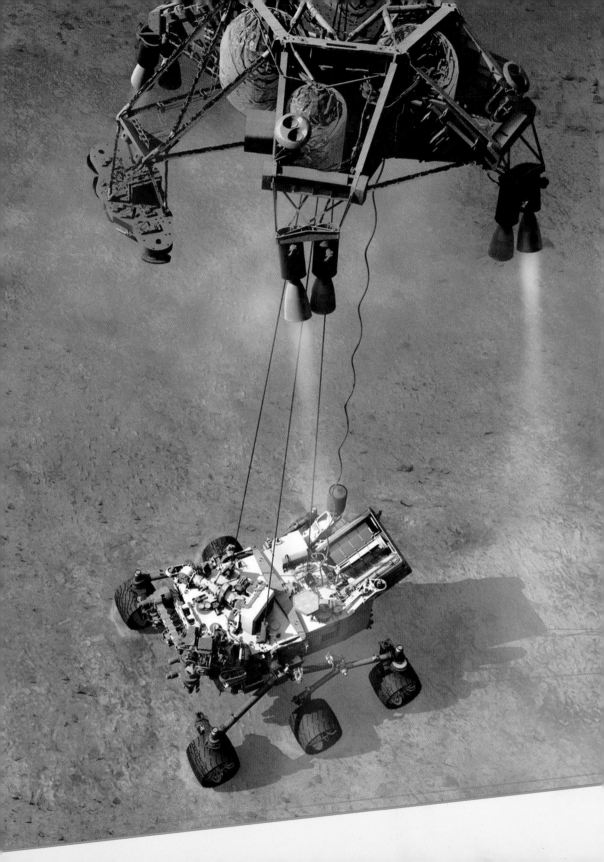

CURIOSITY ON THE RED PLANET

"If any one thing doesn't work just right, it's 'game over,'" said engineer Tom Rivellini. It was August 5, 2012. Approximately 353 million miles (568 million km) from Earth, a spacecraft was nearing Mars. It was following a specific landing plan. The mission team knew it had only one chance. If something went wrong, nothing could be done to fix it.

The robotic *Curiosity* rover dropped to the Martian surface in August 2012.

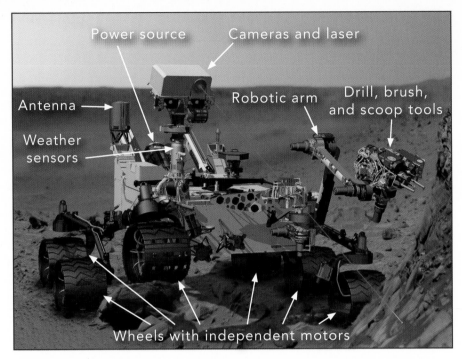

Power source

Cameras and laser

Antenna

Robotic arm

Drill, brush, and scoop tools

Weather sensors

Wheels with independent motors

Curiosity Rover

This diagram shows some of the parts of *Curiosity*. Read about all the described parts of the rover. What parts does *Curiosity* have in common with other robots you have seen?

Inside the spacecraft was the Mars rover *Curiosity*. It had launched from Florida on the morning of November 26, 2011. *Curiosity* was not the first Mars rover. However, it is by far the biggest and most advanced. It is the size of a small car. *Curiosity* is a robotic mobile science laboratory. Its mission is to learn more about Mars.

This was not just any robot. *Curiosity* has many instruments. It uses them for all kinds of tasks. Its laser blasts rocks so their insides can be studied. Sensors record the Martian weather. Cameras and computers let it drive safely on Mars's rocky surface. But before it could study Mars, *Curiosity* had to land safely.

The mission team held its breath. Finally, the rover sent a signal. It had landed successfully. Its eight-month journey was over. The team erupted in cheers. On August 6, 2012, *Curiosity* opened a

IN THE REAL WORLD

Talking Heads

Today some robots can mimic people. They can even hold simple conversations. One robot, developed in Texas, is a head called Han. Working together, its cameras and computers can recognize faces it has seen before. Han can guess people's age and gender from looking at them. It can also guess if they are happy or sad. Then it can react appropriately. Han may be useful for customer service jobs.

new door in space exploration. In 2015 the rover was still exploring Mars.

What Is a Robot?

A robot is a machine that can perform tasks. Some robots follow the instructions of a human. Others decide what to do on their own. Robots that do this are said to have artificial intelligence.

Most robots have certain things in common. They are able to power and move themselves. They can sense their surroundings. They detect light, pressure, or sound. Finally, a robot has to be smart. Programmers create software for the robot to use. This software

Animal Inspiration

Animals inspire many robot designs. Copying the way an animal works is called biomimicry. Some robots swim like fish. They are used to find pollution in the ocean. They can lure real fish away from dangers such as oil spills. One medical robot is shaped like a snake. It can help surgeons access hard-to-reach areas. Snakelike robots have also been used for rescues and exploration. Other robots fly like dragonflies or run like cheetahs.

Some military robots carry heavy loads for soldiers in the field.

tells the robot how to behave. A computer inside the robot runs the software.

Curiosity is one of many robots that work in dangerous places. Some robots work underwater. They explore the seafloor or search for shipwrecks. Others robots work inside active volcanoes. Still more work in factories or in the military.

Many of today's robots work in safer places too. Some help perform surgeries in hospitals. Many people have robots inside their homes. They vacuum

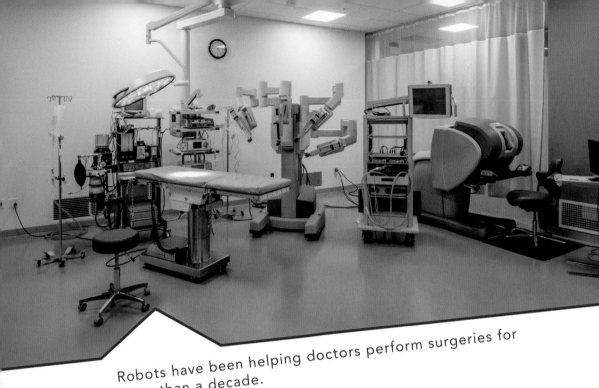

Robots have been helping doctors perform surgeries for more than a decade.

floors and do other chores. Overall, there are more than 1 million robots working in the world today.

A Team Effort

Creating robots requires many skills. Robot makers must know physics and computer science. They need to study engineering and math. Some types of robots involve chemistry and biology. Building surgery robots requires medical knowledge.

The field of making and studying robots is called robotics. This industry is exciting and challenging.

Some creative innovators work alone. But most robots are designed by talented teams. People who work with robots are known as roboticists.

EXPLORE ONLINE

Chapter One discusses the jobs that robots do. It also talks about the people who make these machines. The website below includes more information about robots. What new information did you find on the website? Did it help you better understand what robots are?

What Is a Robot?
mycorelibrary.com/robotics

CHAPTER TWO

A TIMELESS FASCINATION WITH ROBOTS

The history of robotics goes back thousands of years. Robot-like machines were mentioned in ancient legends. Stories spoke of mechanical servants. People talked about clay figures that fought enemies.

During the first century CE, Heron of Alexandria described machines similar to robots. He wrote about mechanical devices. They included clocks and

One of Heron's inventions was a device that spun a ball using steam power.

coin-operated machines. Some early devices were used for entertainment. Engineers created mechanical puppets, musicians, and dancers.

Nikola Tesla's radio-controlled boat is considered to be among the first modern robots. The invention was made public in 1898. A wireless transmitter made the boat move and flash its lights. However, Tesla's boat was not a true robot. It was unable to perform planned tasks or make decisions for itself.

The First Modern Robots

The word *robot* came from the Czech play *Rossum's Universal Robots*. Karel

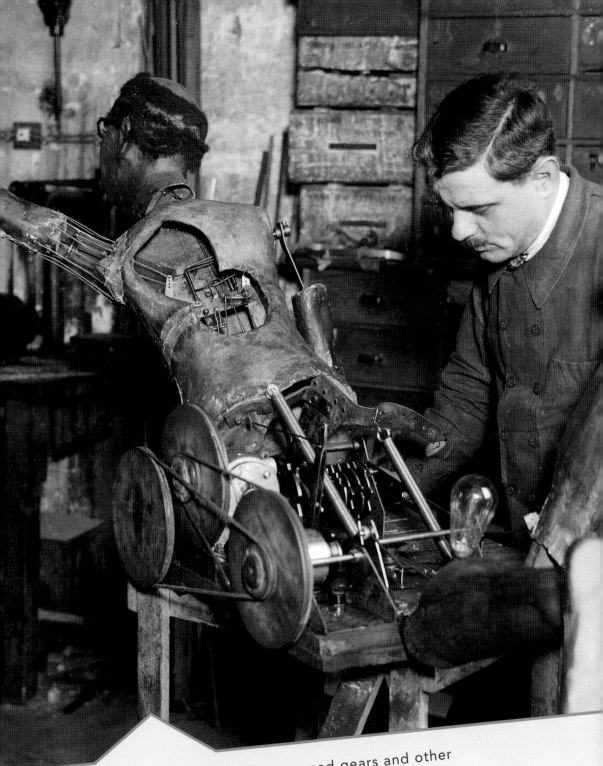

Early robot-like inventions used gears and other mechanical parts to move and function.

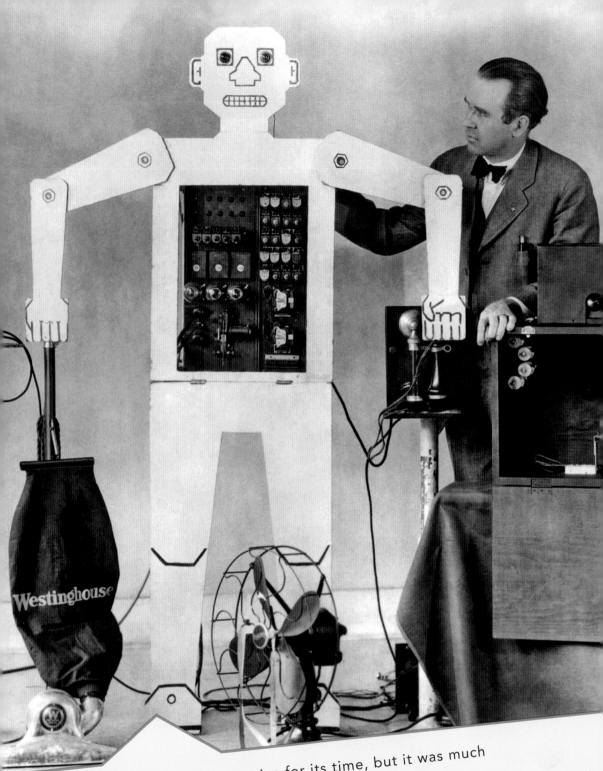

Televox was impressive for its time, but it was much more primitive than today's robots.

Capek and his brother, Josef, wrote the play in 1920. The brothers wanted a name for the artificial creatures in their story. They used *roboti*, which came from the Czech word *robota*, meaning forced labor.

In the early 1900s, real-life robot technology lagged far behind the visions of writers. Rather than doing useful work, many simple robots became marketing tools. Joseph Barnett was an engineer who worked for the company Westinghouse. His company made a device called a Televox. It could operate telephones and switches. In 1927 Barnett

The Story of Robotics

Robots have long been popular characters in stories. Science-fiction writer Isaac Asimov came up with the word *robotics* in his 1942 short story "Runaround." He later used robots in many of his books. Fictional robots appeared in movies long before the invention of real robots. Examples of these appear in such films as *The Master Mystery* (1919), *Metropolis* (1927), and *Forbidden Planet* (1956). These fictional robots were often shown as cruel or controlled by evil scientists.

added a head, arms, body and legs to it. The robot was also named Televox. It was able to buzz, grunt, wave its arms, and even say a few sentences. Televox and other robots were used to advertise the company. They could sit, stand, speak, and perform tricks. They did not have artificial intelligence. Instead they relied on recorded data to operate. But they gave the public a look at the future of robots.

Robots in Manufacturing

In 1954 George Devol and Joseph Engelberger designed the first industrial robot. It was called Unimate. This robotic arm could weld and do other tasks in car factories. More robots were soon designed for use in mass production. They could work at the same task for hours. They never got bored, injured, or tired.

New advances in robotics came quickly after the introduction of Unimate. Researchers at Stanford University invented Shakey the Robot in 1966. It could push blocks through doorways. Shakey used

Shakey got its name from the way it shook back and forth while moving.

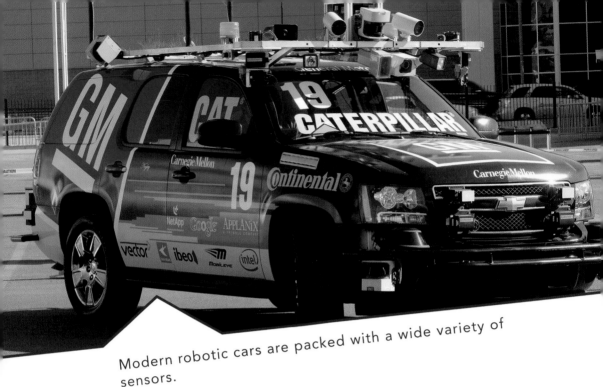

Modern robotic cars are packed with a wide variety of sensors.

a camera to map its surroundings. It then used this information to decide how to push the block. Shakey repeatedly examined the area around itself and made corrections.

Shakey is an example of an autonomous robot. These robots can act without someone controlling them. They observe their environments and take action based on what they find. For instance, robot vacuum cleaners detect obstacles and steer around them.

Smart Bots

In recent decades, roboticists have made robots smarter. New sensors can see a robot's surroundings more clearly. Other sensors detect smells, tastes, or sounds. Computers have gotten smaller and more powerful. This means smart robots can be made smaller than ever before.

Today the world of robots continues to expand quickly. The robotics field has created many job opportunities. People with all kinds of skills and interests have become involved in robotics.

FURTHER EVIDENCE

What was one of the main points of this chapter? What evidence from this chapter supports the point? Below is another source that discusses robotics. Did you learn more about the main point by reading the information presented there? Does the information on this website support the main point? Does it present new evidence?

How Robots Work

mycorelibrary.com/robotics

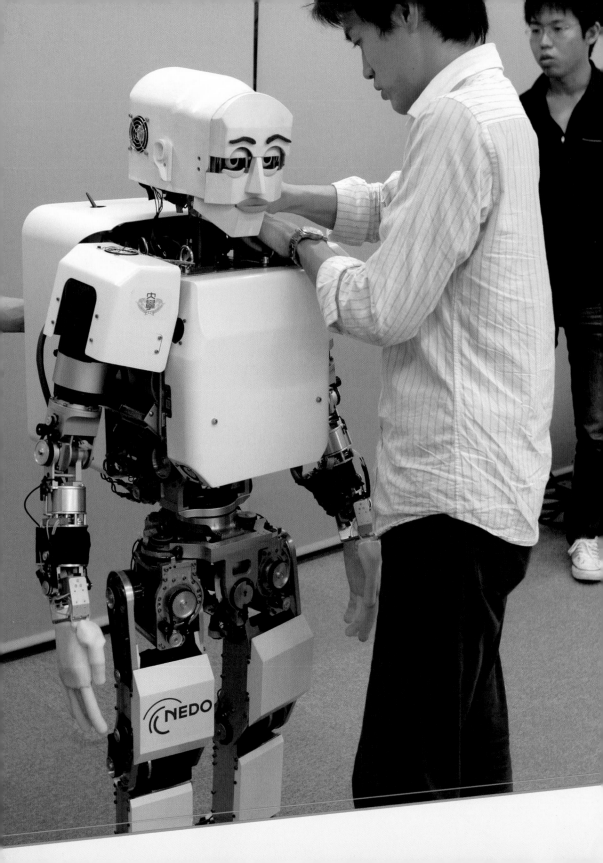

CHAPTER THREE

CAREERS IN ROBOTICS

The field of robotics includes many different types of professionals. Designers come up with ideas for robots. Computer scientists design programs that will tell the robots how to think. Programmers write out these programs in computer code. However, the two most important jobs in robotics belong to engineers and technicians.

The number of careers for those who design, build, and repair robots is growing quickly.

Computer software makes it easy for robot engineers to quickly design and test new robots.

These workers create, use, and repair the millions of robots in existence today.

Engineers

Robotics companies employ several kinds of engineers. Mechanical engineers design the robots' structures. Electrical engineers work with the electrical systems inside the robot. They make sure the robot has enough electricity to work. They connect the different parts of the robot.

The work of a robotics engineer begins with a problem that needs to be solved. Perhaps the government needs a robot that can survive harsh conditions in outer space. A company may want a robot that can safely mow a lawn. The military might seek a rugged robot that can defuse bombs. Engineers know what materials and designs can best solve these problems.

The engineer works with designers to plan the new robot. They usually use a computer. Computer-aided design and drafting (CADD) programs are used to make three-dimensional images of the robot.

IN THE REAL WORLD

A Young Roboticist

When Easton LaChappelle was 14 years old, he built a robotic hand out of LEGO bricks, fishing line, and motors. Easton learned from the Internet how to get the mechanical hand to open and close its fingers. His invention took third place at the 2011 Colorado state science fair. A few years later, Easton invented an inexpensive robotic arm. He even started his own robotics company.

National Robotics Week

In March 2010, the second full week in April was named National Robotics Week in the United States. Its purpose is to celebrate US efforts in robotics. It is also designed to educate and inspire students, researchers, and the public. National Robotics Week involves events all over the country. At these events, people learn important robotics concepts. Activities show the impact robots will have on our future.

Computer-aided manufacturing (CAM) programs can quickly build parts for testing.

Rich Hooper is a robot engineer. On a typical workday he spends a few hours designing electrical systems. He also works with younger engineers, teaching them about what he does. Hooper puts together bills of materials (BOMs). BOMs list all the parts needed to build a robot. These lists, along with CADD drawings, are given to the people who manufacture the robot. Hooper also spends time in meetings, on the phone, and writing e-mails. He believes the field of robotics will continue growing in the future. In 2014 the average salary for a robotics engineer was about $75,000 a year.

Technicians

The job of robot technicians is to build, program, test, install, and repair robots. They need knowledge of circuits, sensors, controllers, and other parts. Technicians must have good mechanical skills. They should to be able to work with their hands.

Robot technicians often travel to support customers. A robot technician discusses any problems with the operators. He or she will adjust sensors, look for damage, and try to locate any other issues. Most robotic systems require frequent adjustments. In 2014 the average salary for a technician was about $55,000 a year.

There are many other jobs in the robotics field. New jobs are being introduced all the time. Robotics is one of the fastest growing industries in the world. It may someday become one of the largest.

Robots that can walk frequently need repairs after falling down.

- Telemarketers: 99.0%
- Umpires and referees: 98.3%
- Cooks: 96.3%
- Janitors: 66.3%
- Programmers: 48.1%
- Judges: 40.1%
- Actors: 37.4%
- Writers: 3.8%
- Preschool teachers: 0.7%

Replaced by Robots

Researchers Carl Benedikt Frey and Michael A. Osborne of the University of Oxford studied which jobs are most likely to be replaced by robots. They compared dozens of careers and assigned each one a percent chance that it would become automated. The researchers considered several key traits, including whether the job required the worker to personally help others and whether the job required the worker to think of clever solutions. Do you agree with the percentages above? What other jobs do you think are more or less likely to be replaced by robots?

Taking Jobs, Creating New Ones

Many people worry about robots taking away jobs from humans. In the late 1900s, many robots took human jobs in car factories. Recently self-checkout lanes have replaced some cashiers. Robots are beginning to serve fast food, work on farms, and even write stories for newspapers. As robots become more advanced, they will be able to work more jobs.

It is clear that robots will change the economy. Workers who are replaced will need to be retrained. However, the rise of the robots also promises to create new jobs. Workers will be needed to design, build, and fix these robots. Schools will need to begin providing more technical training to prepare these workers for the future. It is not clear whether robotics technology will create more jobs than it replaces.

In a 2014 report on the issues surrounding robots in the workplace, the law firm Littler Mendelson explained the impact of robotics:

> Many existing jobs will be automated in the next 20 years. Several repetitive, low-skilled jobs are already being supplanted by technology. However, a number of studies have found that in the aggregate, the robotics industry is creating more jobs than robots replace. For example, the International Federation of Robotics (IFR) estimates that robotics directly created four to six million jobs through 2011, with the total rising to eight to 10 million if indirect jobs are counted. The IFR projects that 1.9 to 3.5 million jobs will be created in the next eight years. Of course, there will be workers displaced as a result of the use of robots, and employers must address the legal rights of such workers.

Source: "The Transformation of the Workplace Through Robotics, Artificial Intelligence, and Automation." The Littler Report. Littler, February 2014. Web. Accessed May 20, 2015.

Changing Minds

Do you have an opinion on whether or not robots should be used in the workplace? Imagine your friend has the opposite opinion. Write a short essay trying to change his or her mind. Include facts and details that support your opinion.

CHAPTER FOUR

WELCOME TO THE FUTURE!

Only a few decades ago, robots were found mainly in books and movies. Today, what was once science fiction has become reality. Robotics has become a huge industry. This industry is growing quickly. What will future generations of roboticists bring to the world? The possibilities seem endless.

Today's amazing robots are the result of decades of research and testing.

Space robots such as *Curiosity* have explored faraway worlds. The military flies robotic planes from thousands of miles away. Researchers are testing robotic cars on US roads. It may not be long before buses, trains, and even airliners will not need human drivers.

The medical field already uses robotics for complex surgeries. Surgical robots cannot yet think for themselves. Trained surgeons control them. Other medical robotics technology is helping injured people

A robot seal named Paro has been used in Japanese nursing homes as a companion for residents.

Agricultural robots may soon change the way the world farms.

walk again. Companies are creating prosthetic limbs that respond to the user's thoughts. Robots are even being used in hospitals as companions to patients. Pharmacist robots may soon give out medication.

There are robots that scrub floors and clean gutters. Robots have even worked as babysitters in retail stores. They watch kids while the adults go shopping.

High-tech Harvesting

More robotic technology is being developed for farming. There are robotic tractors and pruners. Robotic helicopters spray crops. Robots maintain vineyards and pull weeds.

One of the most advanced farming robots is the AGROBOT. Developed by a Spanish robotics company, it is used to pick strawberries. First it lowers a camera into the strawberry bed. A computer analyzes the images the camera collects. It measures color and shape to determine if each berry is ripe. When it finds a ripe berry, the robot's arm places

Robot Delivery

In 2013 Internet shopping company Amazon.com proposed a plan it called Prime Air. This new delivery system would use robotic aircraft to deliver packages to customers. Amazon's robots are designed to fly faster than 50 miles per hour (80 kmh) while carrying 5-pound (2.3-kg) packages. As of spring 2015, Amazon was banned from making deliveries with these robots. The government still needed to pass laws to regulate their safe use.

a basket beneath the berry. The robot slices the berry's stem. The strawberry falls into the basket. Together these steps take approximately four seconds per berry.

Artificial Intelligence and Social Robotics

Robots that people can interact with are also becoming more common. This is one of the most exciting parts of robotics. Robots with social abilities have already been used to work with people. For example, people with autism sometimes have a difficult time talking to others. They may have an easier time interacting with a robot.

Robotic drones may one day deliver packages to your front door.

Some roboticists try to make social robots look and act like humans. However, even a robotic-looking machine can form a bond with people. Soldiers once picked up the shattered remains of a bomb-disposal robot and asked for it to be fixed. A repair shop offered to give them a new one. But the soldiers said they wanted to keep using the one they knew. It had saved their lives.

Robots seem destined to play a large role in our future. In the last few decades, computers have gone from laboratories to workplaces to people's homes. Robots have begun to do the same. The field of robotics is projected to grow dramatically in the future. Students who begin studying robots today can become the pioneering robot scientists of tomorrow.

Patrick Lin, an editor of *Robot Ethics: The Ethical and Social Implications of Robotics*, writes:

> *Some robots are miniature today and ever shrinking, perhaps bringing to life the idea of a "nanobot," swarms of which might work inside our bodies or in the atmosphere or cleaning up oil spills. Even rooms or entire buildings might be considered as robots—beyond the "smart homes" of today—if they can manipulate the environment in ways more significant than turning on lights and air conditioning. With synthetic biology, cognitive science, and nanoelectronics, future robots could be biologically based. And human-machine integrations, that is, cyborgs, may be much more prevalent than they are today, which are mostly limited to patients with artificial body parts, such as limbs and joints that are controlled to some degree by robotics. . . . What we intuitively consider as robots today may change, given different form factors and materials of tomorrow.*

Source: Patrick Lin, Keith Abney, and George A. Bekey. Robot Ethics: The Ethical and Social Implications of Robotics. *Cambridge, MA: MIT Press, 2011. Google eBook. 6.*

What's the Big Idea?

Read the text carefully. What is the main idea? What details did the author use to support the main idea? How does Lin view the future of robotics? Do you agree with his vision of the future?

FAST FACTS

- The earliest robots were mechanical devices. Today's robots involve complex electronics, sensors, computers, and software.

- People sometimes use robots for work that is too dangerous, difficult, dirty, or just plain boring for humans to do.

- There are more than 1 million robots working in the world today.

- Designing, constructing, and testing robots uses a combination of physics, computer science, mechanical engineering, electrical engineering, structural engineering, and mathematics.

- Robots may replace some existing jobs, but they are likely to create others.

- There are jobs in robotics for designers, programmers, software engineers, automation technicians, account management experts, and field service technicians. There are also jobs in sales, testing, and maintenance.

- Robotics engineers use computer-aided design and drafting (CADD) and computer-aided manufacturing (CAM) programs for research and design.

Dig Deeper

After reading this book, what questions do you still have about a job in robotics? With an adult's help, find a few reliable sources to see what jobs are available today and what kind of education you might need. Write a paragraph about what you learned.

You Are There

This book told about the Mars rover *Curiosity*. Ask a librarian or other adult to help you find the latest news about what *Curiosity* has told us about Mars. How has this robot improved our understanding of Mars? Imagine you are on Mars watching *Curiosity* explore. Write a letter home telling your friends what you are seeing. Be sure to add plenty of detail.

Surprise Me

Chapter Two talked about the history of robots and robotics. What two or three things surprised you about how long people have been thinking about and designing robots? Why did you find those things surprising?

Tell the Tale

In Chapter Three, you read about National Robotics Week. Ask an adult to help you find more information about this event. Write 200 words about what you hope to learn during the next celebration. What kinds of events would you like to attend? What activities would interest you?

GLOSSARY

autonomous
acting independently or having the freedom to do so

mechanical
having to do with machines or tools

prosthetic
an artificial body part, such as a leg or hand

prototype
a model of a new product or device used for testing

repetitive
being repeated

rover
a robot that travels on the surface of a planet or moon

sensor
an instrument that can detect changes in things such as heat, sound, or pressure, and send the information to a controller

technology
the use of science and engineering to do practical things

LEARN MORE

Books

Ceceri, Kathy. *Robotics: Discover the Science and Technology of the Future with 20 Projects.* White River Junction, VT: Nomad Press, 2012.

Mara, Wil. *Robotics: From Concept to Consumer.* New York: Scholastic, 2015.

Websites

To learn more about STEM in the Real World, visit **booklinks.abdopublishing.com.** These links are routinely monitored and updated to provide the most current information available.

Visit **mycorelibrary.com** for free additional tools for teachers and students.

INDEX

ABOUT THE AUTHOR

Robin Koontz is a freelance author of a wide variety of nonfiction and fiction books for children and young adults. Raised in Maryland and Alabama, Robin lives with her husband in the Coast Range of western Oregon.